D1080392

LIVING FOR THE *FUTURE*

WORLD FOOD

Sally Morgan and Pauline Lalor

FRANKLIN WATTS
NEW YORK • LONDON • SYDNEY

Most of our everyday activities, whether turning on a light or taking a trip in a car, use up some of the earth's resources. These resources will not last forever, yet we continue to need and use them in our daily lives.

In June 1992, the largest ever political meeting in history was held – the United Nations Conference on Environment and Development (UNCED), or the 'Earth Summit'. Politicians, environmental experts and many others gathered together to discuss the challenge that humanity faces as we move towards the twenty-first century. How can we live our lives in a way that suits us, but without using up the resources that our children in turn will need to live their lives?

Agenda 21 is the document that was produced as a result of the Earth Summit. It sets out a practical plan for every nation to follow to achieve 'sustainable development'. This means not only allowing us to live the lives we want to lead, but allowing everyone else to live a comfortable life, while also protecting our environment for future generations.

© 1997 Franklin Watts
96 Leonard Street
London
EC2A 4RH

Franklin Watts Australia
14 Mars Road
Lane Cove
NSW 2066

ISBN 0 7496 2854 5

Dewey Decimal Classification Number 338.1

A CIP catalogue record for this book is available from the British Library

Series editor: Helen Lanz
Cover and series designer: Kirstie Billingham
Picture researcher: Sue Mennell
Consultant: Niall Marriott, a founder of Living Earth Foundation and consultant in environmental, community and educational issues

Printed in the United Kingdom

Picture credits
Cover images: Still Pictures/Mark Edwards; Rex Features

Bruce Coleman Ltd. 25b (Joe Macdonald); Ecoscene 18b (Chinch Gryniewicz), *20b* (Sally Morgan), 26t (Lees), 28t (Anthony Cooper); E.T. Archive 2lb (*Scene in Irish Cabin* by Erskine Nichol/Sheffield City Art Galleries); Eye Ubiquitous 4l (Dave Fobister), 7t (E.L. Neil), 9t (David Cumming), 14t (T. Nottingham); Robert Harding 27t; Hutchison Library 4t (Sarah Errington), 18t (Robert Aberman), 20m (J.C.Tordai), 28b (Crispin Hughes); Massey Ferguson Ltd., Coventry 6t, 14b; NHPA 16b (David Woodfall), 17m (N.A. Callow), 19b (Anthony Bannister), 22b (E.A. Janes); Panos Pictures 5t (Dominic Harcourt-Webster), 5b (Penny Tweedie), 9b (Jim Holmes), 11b (Howard Davies), 13t (Jean-Leo Dugast), 13b (Jean-Leo Dugast), 17t (Chris Stowers), 19t (Sean Sprague), 20t (Sean Sprague) 22t (Nick Robinson), 23t (Jim Holmes), 24t (Thomas Raupach), 24b (Betty Press), 29b (Sean Sprague); Popperfoto 8t (Eric Ferferberg); Rex Features 29t (Sipa Press); Frank Spooner/Gamma 25t (Murdo Macleod); Still Pictures 4br (Jim Wark), 6b (Jim Wark), 7b (Paul Harrison), 8b (Jorgen Schytte), 10t (Nigel Dickinson), 10b (Mark Edwards), 12 (John Paul Kay), 15t (Edward Parker), 15b (Stephen Pern), 16t (Kent Wood), 17b (Herbert Girardet), 2lt (Nigel Dickinson), 24t (Thomas Raupach), 26m (Alain Compost), 26b (Mark Edwards), 27b (Andre Maslennikor), 28m (Mark Edwards); Topham Picture-Point/ Associated Press 1lt.

CONTENTS

FOOD FOR LIFE 4

FARMING TODAY 6

ACTION PLAN TO FEED THE WORLD 10

THINKING GREEN 14

WATER FOR LIFE 18

MORE VARIETY 20

GETTING FOOD TO MARKET 26

THE WAY AHEAD 28

GLOSSARY / FURTHER INFORMATION 30

INDEX 32

Everyone in the world needs food! We all need to eat food in order to stay alive and healthy. To be healthy, we must eat a mixture of different foods to give us a balanced diet. Sweet, starchy, fatty and oily foods give us energy for movement and warmth. Meat, fish, eggs, peas and beans contain protein, which helps us grow and repair our bodies. Fruit, vegetables, wholemeal bread, fish, liver and milk give us vitamins and minerals for good health.

Young children need a healthy diet.

FOOD FOR LIFE

FOOD AROUND THE WORLD

The world's food is produced by the farming industry. Our food comes mostly from plants and animals. In different parts of the world, the weather and soil affect the type of crops grown and the type of animals kept on farms.

'Children need to understand about their own need for food and their global participation is of the utmost importance.'

AGENDA 21

Much of the farm land of North America is used to grow cereal crops. Land is also needed to graze beef and dairy cattle.

KEEPING THE BALANCE

Today, one-third of the earth's land surface is used for farming. People started to cultivate, or work, the soil more than 9,000 years ago. From this moment, they began to alter their surroundings – the environment. In recent times, modern farming methods and the growing demands made on the land have damaged the environment. The demand for farm land is increasing and, every year, forest and grassland disappear to make way for crops.

The removal of natural vegetation results in soil erosion, where the exposed soil dries out and is blown away.

Land is needed for farming, but some countryside should remain.

We have to decide how much land is to be given over to farming and how much is going to be left untouched for wildlife.

'We do not inherit the earth from our fathers, we borrow it from our children.'

We must be very careful not to damage the delicate balance of the earth and the environment in our search to find ways of making more food.

Farming is probably the biggest industry in the world today. Until the 1950s, the world's farmers produced more crops every year by simply using more land. Nowadays, bigger harvests are produced by using advances in technology and new farming methods. These include the use of high-tech machinery, chemicals and specializing in one specific area of farming.

Machinery has dramatically changed farming methods.

FARMING TODAY

MODERN FARMING

One of the most efficient ways of farming is to clear the natural vegetation of trees, grasses and other plants to create huge fields, planted with just one type of crop year after year. Cereals, such as wheat, are often grown this way. Modern machinery available in developed parts of the world, such as the United States, Australasia and Europe, has made this style of farming easy and effective. But vast areas of one crop destroy the natural balance of the environment.

'Farming must be improved to meet the demands of the future without expanding on to natural lands and damaging fragile ecosystems.'

AGENDA 21

Growing just one crop affects the chemicals in the soil.

Plants need nutrients if they are to grow well, so many farmers add fertilizers to the soil where their crops grow. Fertilizers help to give a better yield, or size of harvest.

Most farmers also use chemicals to kill pests, such as insects and weeds, and to fight diseases which harm crops. These fertilizers and chemicals can wash off the land and pollute the waterways, air and even the food they are 'helping' to grow.

Crops may be sprayed several times during the growing season to maximize the yield.

CASE STUDY

THE ISSUES AT STAKE

THE DDT DISASTER

DDT is an insecticide. During the 1950s and 1960s, DDT was sprayed on crops all around the world to kill insect pests. Before this, DDT had been tested by scientists and was found to be harmless to humans. But nobody had realized that the amount of DDT would build up as it passed along the food chain, from the sprayed plants to the animals that ate them. Seed-eating birds died in their thousands after eating seed which had been sprayed by DDT. People eating DDT-contaminated food became very ill. Although DDT has now been banned in most countries for almost 30 years, it can still be found in the environment.

Scientists have to check fully the effect of new pesticides before allowing them to be used on farms.

RICH VS POOR

Farming in developing countries, such as Africa, Asia and South America, is very different from farming in developed nations. Because there are few machines, such as tractors, and because chemicals are expensive, the crops are often poor. Farmers use traditional methods of farming which are in balance with the environment. However, this type of farming often only provides enough food for the farmer and his family to survive, and supplies little food for other families.

In the poorer countries of Asia, Africa and South America, nearly half the population just barely survive. One in every five people suffers from malnutrition.

CASE STUDY

THE SAN LORENZO COMMUNITY, HONDURAS

WORKING TOGETHER

In Lempira, Honduras, the women and children from the San Lorenzo community work together to prepare the land for planting. Members grow enough maize, beans and other vegetables to feed the 500 people of the community. They have shown that, if they all work together using traditional methods, no-one need go hungry.

When using traditional farming methods, more food can be produced if people work together.

A FAIR DEAL?

Sometimes, people from large companies in wealthier nations visit the developing countries to buy the better farm land there. This land is usually much less expensive than land in the developed countries. Local people cannot afford to bid against the large companies, so they are forced to use land that is not suitable for farming. This makes it harder for the local people to feed themselves.

PROCESSING AND PACKAGING

Wherever food is grown, some foods, such as fruit and vegetables, are not much different when we eat them from how they are when they are growing. Most of our food, however, has been altered, or processed, in some way. It may have been dried or frozen to make it last longer.

This preservation of food often uses chemical processes. Also, much of the food on sale in the developed world is sold in packaging to keep it fresh.

Many people are used to seeing brightly packaged, processed foods from all corners of the world, but perhaps we should start thinking about the cost to the environment.

(Above) No packaging in sight! Although some packaging can help to keep food fresh, energy and resources could be saved if it was kept to a minimum, rather than having many layers (left).

The world is faced with a huge problem. The human population is increasing all the time. With so many mouths to feed, it is becoming more and more difficult to make sure that no one goes hungry. In the developed world, where the population is growing slowly, food is plentiful. It is in the poorest countries, where there is the greatest population increase, that the food supply and its distribution are limited.

ACTION PLAN TO FEED THE WORLD

PLAN FOR THE 21ST CENTURY

In June 1992, Rio de Janeiro in Brazil hosted the United Nations Conference on Environment and Development. It was called the Earth Summit. Representatives of almost every country discussed the problems that the world is facing, asking how the earth can be protected when we all depend on it to sustain our lifestyles.

One very important subject of discussion was sustainable development, something which affects all our futures.

Delegates at UNCED discussed ways of producing more food while protecting the environment.

A sustainable society is one which can keep up its standard of living into the future. The world environment is being damaged and resources are being used up ever more rapidly. Somehow, we have to make changes to our lives so that we can protect the environment. We must conserve resources so that they are available for future generations as well as present ones. There has to be a balance between the needs of the people and nature itself. And this requires good management.

We have to find ways of sharing out fairly the world's food resources.

Today, the world produces enough food to feed everyone – yet, every night, 700 million people, or 1 in 6 of the world's population, go to bed hungry.

THE RIGHT TO FOOD

The world population is increasing by more than 90 million people every year. The food that is available today needs to be shared out more evenly across the globe. However, the grain harvest throughout the world is gradually slowing down. Farmers have to produce more food, but from existing farm land – we cannot afford to lose more natural habitats. The environment must not be forgotten.

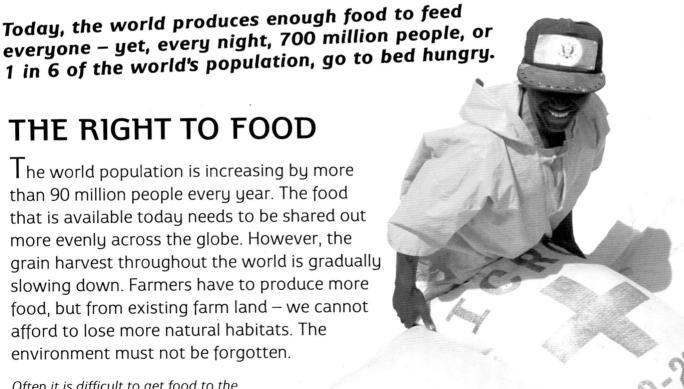

Often it is difficult to get food to the people who need it. Better ways of managing and distributing world food need to be found.

NEW TECHNOLOGY

Scientists and governments must make sure that new ideas and methods of farming are spread throughout the whole world. In this way, farming can be improved everywhere. At the moment, most new technical developments are found only in the rich developed countries. They must be spread into the developing world, and not be used only by the rich nations.

The new technologies that farmers are encouraged to use must be appropriate to the farmers' local environment.

AGENDA 21

Here are some of the most important aims of Agenda 21 concerning food, including our need for water:

- encourage more environmentally sensitive methods of farming with better harvests but fewer chemicals
- promote good use of water resources
- prevent the over-fishing of the oceans
- provide everyone with a greater variety of food
- protect plants and animals for future generations
- save energy and reduce waste when processing and transporting food
- give the right kind of aid to help the hungry of the world

'Everybody has the right to a standard of living good enough for the health and well-being of himself and of his family, including food.'

Universal Declaration of Human Rights, 1948

Rice is probably the world's most important food crop. It is eaten every day by more than 3 billion people.

ENVIRONMENTALLY SENSITIVE FARMING

Almost half the people in the world eat rice every day. Rice is grown in India, China and Southeast Asia using methods that have changed little for hundreds of years. In most rice fields the soil is turned over using ploughs which are pulled by animals. Much of the sowing, planting, weeding and harvesting is done by hand. Manure from animals and people is used as a fertilizer. Growing rice in this way does not cause as much damage to the environment as the intensive farming of other cereals such as wheat.

Thinning the rice plants to allow room for growth is important.

- use more environmentally sensitive farming
- produce more yield at less cost
- use fewer chemicals
- use better pest control

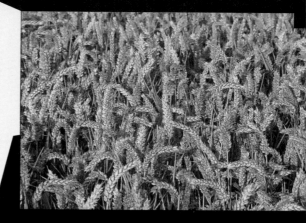

THINKING GREEN

Humans are altering the earth's atmosphere, soil and oceans with pollution from agriculture and industry. It is really important that we realize that we must live in harmony with our planet in order to survive. We must 'think green', while avoiding the mistakes made in the so-called 'Green Revolution'.

THE GREEN REVOLUTION

In the 1960s and 1970s, food production was increased to help the starving people of the world. Farmers were encouraged to produce bigger harvests by growing new and improved varieties of cereals. But these new varieties needed heavy fertilization and increased use of pesticides.

The Green Revolution managed to produce more food on the same amount of land. But this was achieved at the expense of both the environment and the economies of developing countries.

Developing countries were encouraged to grow these new 'wonder crops', but they soon found that they had to buy the fertilizers and pesticides from the richer developed countries. This caused them to build up a 'foreign debt' – money they owed to the richer countries which they could not afford to pay. Though more food was produced during this period, it was not a success in terms of the environment or the economies (or wealth) of the poorer countries.

TRADITIONAL METHODS – THE WAY FORWARD?

Now in developing countries, traditional methods are being improved. The farmers have learnt over generations which plants are best suited to the local soil and climate. The 'improved' maize plants developed during the Green Revolution are badly affected by drought and have proved not to be suitable for growing in hot countries. Scientists are now looking at ways of improving traditional crops, such as millet and sorghum, which are more resistant to drought.

Manioc, or cassava, is a staple food in South America. It is a traditional crop, well suited to local conditions.

CASE STUDY

THE NOMADS IN MONGOLIA

A TRADITIONAL AND SELF-SUFFICIENT WAY OF LIFE

The nomadic travelling people who live high on the barren plains of Mongolia breed herds of yak, sheep and cattle in summer to provide meat in winter. There are few plants, so these people rely on meat. The animals can only graze in summer, though a few can be kept on stored food over the winter. Nothing is wasted, and every bit of the animal is used, including its dung. This can be used as a cooking fuel as there are few trees for wood.

The conditions on the Mongolian plains are tough and the nomads rely on animals for their food.

FEWER CHEMICALS

Modern farming methods in developed countries have become dependent on the type of chemicals introduced during the Green Revolution. They rely on pesticides to kill the pests, fungicides to stop fungal diseases, herbicides to kill weeds, and fertilizers to increase yields. However, these chemicals are harming wildlife, the environment and people's health. There are other ways of farming, though, which make use of natural substances to control disease and fertilize the soil.

Farmers spray pesticides to rid their crops of pests that damage the plants.

NATURAL FERTILIZERS

In a natural habitat, when plants die they are broken down and the nutrients are returned to the soil to be used again. This is natural recycling. As crops grow, they take nutrients from the soil, and when the crops are harvested these nutrients are removed from the soil permanently. This is why farmers add fertilizers. But there are natural sources of fertilizer that could be used, such as animal manure, compost, used hops from the brewing industry and even human 'manure'!

Sewage is rich in nutrients. Like hops and compost it is also a renewable resource, in that it will not run out. When it is treated correctly, sewage sludge can be spread on the land as a natural fertilizer.

NATURAL PEST CONTROL

Pests can ruin crops. There are ways of controlling pests without using pesticides, which often kill animals or insects that control pests naturally. For example, greenfly is a pest that eats plants such as wheat. But ladybirds and hover fly larvae eat greenfly. Keeping hedgerows and scrub, or rough areas of land, around fields is important. This is where many of the predators live, including ladybirds. Farmers need to encourage such natural predators to settle around their crops.

Swarms of locusts devastate vast areas of crops each year in Africa. A whole crop can be consumed in just a few hours.

There are some new varieties of crops which are naturally resistant to pests. This means that pesticides do not have to be used at all.

CASE STUDY

KEW GARDENS, UK

KEW GOES GREEN

Kew Gardens, in London, has many large tropical glass houses containing collections of different types of plants. It is not surprising that the plants are attacked by pests, especially the mealy bug. This bug is a small insect which sucks the sap from plant stems, leaving a sticky mess on the plant. But Kew has avoided using pesticides. Since 1992, it has used lizards and ladybirds instead because they eat mealy bugs as part of their diet.

Kew is an important store for many plant species.

AGENDA 21 **aims to:**

- save, store and recycle water
- irrigate, or water, crops
- reduce water pollution
- manage fish stocks

Careful irrigation can save water.

WATER FOR LIFE

Water is vital. Without it, there would be no life on earth. But there is only a limited supply. In developed countries, people believe that clean water is plentiful – endlessly available when you turn on a tap. But in the developing world drought is a common cause of famine. All farming relies on water, so this essential resource must be conserved and recycled, and must not be polluted.

Just keeping all the farm animals in the world alive uses 60 billion litres of water each day, that is enough to fill 120,000 full-size swimming pools.

CASE STUDY

BAOBAB FARM, KENYA

RECYCLING WATER SUPPLIES

Baobab farm is a flourishing farm that uses sustainable methods. Each year, Baobab farm produces 35 tonnes of fish. The tilapia fish are grown in ponds. The fish quickly dirty the water. Because water supplies are limited, the water cannot be wasted. It must be cleaned and recycled. The dirty water flows through special troughs in which crop plants are grown. The plants absorb the nutrients from the waste water, cleaning it so that it can be used for the fish again.

Dirty fish water is piped to beds of rice plants.

Drip irrigation takes the water directly to the plants so less water is wasted.

BRINGING WATER TO THE DESERT

In the drier parts of the world, crops have to be irrigated – watered artificially – because there is not enough rain. Water is used from rivers and wells. This allows farmers to grow crops where they would not normally survive. But irrigation can be very wasteful, with much water being lost through leaks and evaporation on its way to the fields. New methods of irrigation are being developed so that, in the future, farmers can irrigate more land using less water.

'Water demands are increasing rapidly, with 70-80% required for irrigation, less than 20% for industry, and a mere 6% for domestic consumption.'

AGENDA 21

OVER FISHING

Many people rely on fish as their main source of protein, so it forms an essential part of the diet. There is a huge demand for fish worldwide and too many are being taken from the sea. One way forward may be a long-term ban on fishing in certain parts of the oceans. This policy has proved not only to protect fish, but to lead to better fishing in the rest of the oceans.

Large fish catches are common in all the oceans, but such fishing needs to be controlled.

- encourage a greater range and variety of foods
- conserve plants and animals

MORE VARIETY

We rely on just a few types of plants and animals to provide most of our food. Most of the world's meat comes from just nine different types of animal – cattle, pigs, sheep, goats, water buffalo, chickens, ducks, geese and turkeys.

(Above and right) Meat forms a big part of many people's diet – over 7,000 million chickens are kept around the world.

Cereals and potatoes form the bulk of people's diets. Cereal crops are so important that they are grown on more than 1/6th of the world's farm land.

We need to reduce our dependency on these animals and cereals and eat a greater variety of foods. Variety is important – if we relied on several crops, the failure of a single crop would not be so important.

LAND USE

A larger variety of foods means that alternative crops can be grown on land that is unsuitable for traditional cereals. Around the world, some land has fallen into non-use because it has been damaged by farming. But this land could be reused for new crop varieties, preserving further country-side from being turned into new agricultural land.

Several varieties of spring barley are being grown in this field. It is important to preserve as many different varieties of cereals as possible.

CASE STUDY

IRELAND

HUNGER IN HISTORY – THE IRISH FAMINE

When we think of hunger, we usually think of people from developing countries. But in Ireland in 1845, almost the entire potato crop was destroyed by a fungal disease. Potatoes were the main food for most of the people and, by 1850, about one-and-a-half million people had died from starvation, and a similar number of people had left Ireland and emigrated to America, Canada and England to get away from the famine. This shows just how dangerous it can be to rely on a single source of food.

THE RIGHT ANIMALS IN THE RIGHT PLACE

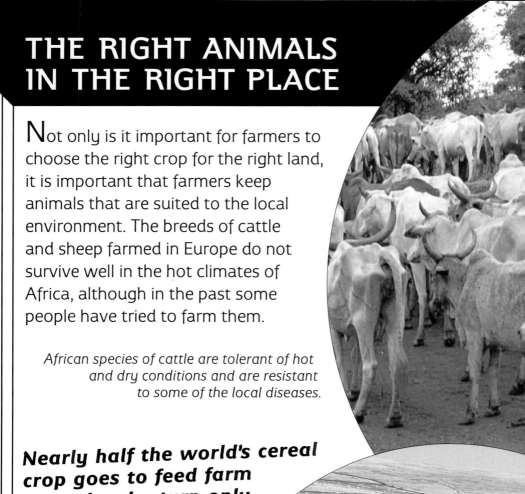

Not only is it important for farmers to choose the right crop for the right land, it is important that farmers keep animals that are suited to the local environment. The breeds of cattle and sheep farmed in Europe do not survive well in the hot climates of Africa, although in the past some people have tried to farm them.

African species of cattle are tolerant of hot and dry conditions and are resistant to some of the local diseases.

Nearly half the world's cereal crop goes to feed farm animals who turn only a small amount of this food into meat.

Not surprisingly, it is the local breeds of animals that do best in local conditions. Animals such as goats and sheep can live on poor land that cannot be used to grow crops. Goats can provide meat, milk and cheese just like cows can.

Swaledale sheep can survive cold winters and are happy grazing the poor quality grass of the upland slopes of Britain.

It is vital to consider the natural environment when deciding on which animals to keep, rather than to import expensive and unsuitable animals from other parts of the world.

(Above) Animals are still transported around the world, sometimes to unsuitable places.

CASE STUDY

EAST AFRICA

GAME RANCHING

Native species such as the eland (a large antelope) look like cattle, but they are wild animals which are adapted to the East African climate. They are resistant to the native pests, unlike European breeds of cattle. Farmers are now finding it more efficient to farm these native species. They make better use of the grass and suffer from fewer diseases. Overall, they are easier to farm and do much less damage to the environment.

Eland grow quickly and provide the farmer with meat and leather.

SCIENCE FICTION BECOMES FACT

Food varieties and the composition (or make-up) of food are areas of interest to scientists as well as farmers. Scientists can now actually change the genetic make-up, (the basic characteristics) of a living organism. This is called genetic engineering. Organisms can be given new abilities and features that they lacked before. Maize plants, for example, have been given a gene that makes them resistant to certain pests and so, it is claimed, maize has become a more reliable crop. Genetic engineering may help us to feed the world's people.

New, genetically engineered crops will allow farmers to grow plants on salty land, for example, or in cold climates or in areas that suffer from drought.

'The important advantage of genetic engineering is that it provides the very latest technology to farmers in a traditional package – the seed.'

Charles S Gesser and Robert T Fraley,
Scientific American, June 1992.

In the past, scientists improved crops and animals by selecting individuals that had the best qualities. This could be a crop that was resistant to pests, for example. These individuals would be used as parents to the next generation. The young plant or animal would then take on the new quality, improving slowly over succeeding generations. Genetic engineering allows scientists to improve crops in a shorter period of time.

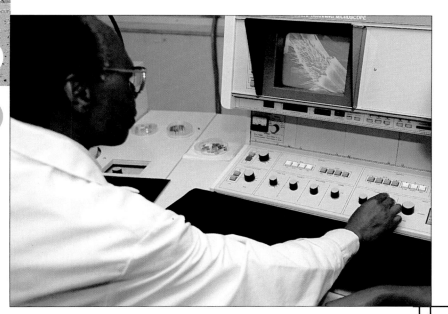

Agenda 21 encourages scientists to make use of new technology in order to research alternative ways of increasing world food.

But there are also dangers involved with growing genetically modified, or altered, foodstuffs. There may be side effects as a result of altering the genetic make-up of a plant or animal which might not be apparent for some time. So caution must be used when genetically altering anything.

By using genetic information from her mother's cell, Dolly, the sheep, was the first ever clone of an adult mammal — she is the exact copy of her mother. It is this technology that scientists feel may contribute to solving some of our food problems.

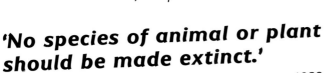

'No species of animal or plant should be made extinct.'
The World Conservation Strategy, 1980.

SAVING ANIMALS AND PLANTS FOR THE FUTURE

Far too many animals and plants are becoming extinct each year. Somehow, we have to conserve as many species as possible. Nowadays farmers tend to use just a few modern varieties of plants and breeds of animals. But the older varieties must be preserved, for they may be useful in the future. For example, they may carry genes which are resistant to diseases that are not a danger today, but which could affect crops or food sources of the future.

More animal and plant species are under threat of extinction because their habitats are being lost — cleared for farm land and new developments. Their loss could have unknown effects.

AGENDA 21 aims to:

- encourage people to eat less processed food
- reduce packaging
- educate more people

GETTING FOOD TO MARKET

In the developing parts of the world, most food is bought fresh, unprocessed and unpackaged from local markets. The food has been grown locally. But it is very different in the developed world. Here, fresh food markets are disappearing and in their place are huge supermarkets. The food is packaged and displayed on shelves.

Packaging has two roles. It keeps the food clean and fresh and it makes the food look good, so people want to buy it. But once unwrapped, the packaging is tossed away and probably ends up in a rubbish dump. Plastic packaging will not rot down, so it stays in the ground for many years. By eating unprocessed and unpackaged foods, we not only help to preserve our environment, but we can also save money and energy.

Processed foods are very convenient, but they use energy and create waste. At each stage of the process, food is wasted and energy used.

TRANSPORTED TO MARKET

Have you ever looked to see where food comes from? Nowadays, food is transported around the world. It is not unusual to eat apples from New Zealand, beans from Kenya and nuts from India. But transportation uses up energy and contributes to air pollution.

Many of us have got used to eating whatever food we want, whenever we want it. It does not matter to us if it is out of season in our country, because we can import the food from elsewhere in the world. We should really think about what we eat and try to eat locally produced goods as much as possible.

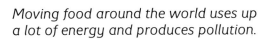

Moving food around the world uses up a lot of energy and produces pollution.

'Most Americans will leave behind a monument of waste some 4,000 times their body weight by the time they die. A European will leave 1,000 times their weight, but a Madagascan will leave just 100 times their body weight.'

From Sex, Lemurs and Holes in the Sky, Central TV Documentary 1992.

CASE STUDY

LOCAL FOOD GROWERS, THE UK

THE LOCAL BOX SCHEMES

In the UK, many organic growers of fruit and vegetables have set up a local box scheme. Each week, households participating in the scheme buy a box of organically grown vegetables – these are grown without using any chemicals. The vegetables vary according to what is in season. This scheme allows the grower of the vegetables to sell direct to the customer with the minimum transportation and packaging.

In this scheme everybody wins – the grower, the customer and the environment.

- think globally (encourage fairer trade between countries)
- eat locally, eat organically

Organic eating is healthy eating!

THE WAY AHEAD

Today there are rich nations with plenty of food and poor nations which are starving. The food resources of the world have to be shared out more fairly. The only way everybody is going to get enough food is to spend money on improving farming. But, for this to work, there has be world peace, financial growth and the removal of the huge debts owed by developing countries.

Developing countries would benefit far more by being helped to improve their own farming methods (above), rather than being given food aid (below).

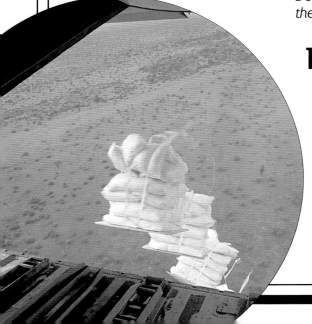

FOOD STORES

Most developed countries have a surplus of food, so they can export food. The European Union (EU) controls food prices to make sure that the countries of the EU never run out of food. As a result, stores of food such as wheat, meat and milk have built up. You might think that this surplus food should be given to the starving people, but it is not that easy.

TRADE NOT AID

Giving developing countries money or food aid only helps in the short term. If money is given, it is often with conditions. For example, in return for the aid, a developing country may have to buy goods from the country providing the help. This forces the developing country to build up enormous foreign debts. To pay these debts, the country might grow 'cash crops', a food which is exported to earn income. If these debts were cancelled, the poorer countries could use their land to grow essential crops to feed their own people. Developing countries must be given a chance to help themselves to make a future.

'It seems that as the rich get richer the poor do get poorer. Is it not time to speak of living together in one world?'

Countries that are at war, such as Rwanda, suffer from food shortages because the people cannot farm the land safely, and food reserves are quickly used up.

TAKING ACTION!

Most governments have plans to tackle the food problems. But everyone of us can make a difference by making simple changes to our daily lives. Try to be aware of what is going on in the world to produce foods. Read the labels to see where food has come from. Try to buy food that has been grown or produced locally. Avoid foods that are heavily packaged and, if you do have waste packaging, try and make sure that as much as possible is recycled. Support your local organic producers. Think globally, eat locally!

GLOSSARY

aid: in this book, help in the form of money or food given to countries in need.

cereal: a grass that produces grain used for food, such as wheat or maize.

clone: an exact copy of a living being, plant or animal, grown from a single cell.

developed country: a country that relies on money from industry and in which factories provide more jobs than agriculture.

developing country: a country that relies on money from agriculture, rather than on manufacturing goods for export, for example.

drought: a period of time when the rains fail and there is a shortage of water.

ecosystem: the network of animals and plants which interact with and depend on each other in a locality.

environment: all the conditions that surround us, including the air, the soil, water, and other animals and plants.

extinct: gone forever or died out.

fertilizer: a substance containing nutrients necessary for healthy plant growth.

food chain: a priority of eating order in nature. It usually starts with plants which are eaten by plant-eating animals which, in turn, are eaten by meat-eating animals.

gene: a unit of biological information, passed from parent to offspring. Each gene controls a characteristic such as eye colour.

genetic engineering: changing the genetic make-up of an organism, usually by adding a gene from another organism.

government: a group of people who run a country, voted in to their jobs by the public.

habitat: the natural living area of a plant or animal, for example a pond or a wood.

herbicide: chemical used to kill weeds.

insecticide: chemical used to kill insect pests.

irrigation: the artificial watering of a crop.

non-renewable: something that cannot be replaced. Once a non-renewable resource, such as oil, is taken from the environment is gone permanently.

nutrient: a chemical substance needed by a plant in order for it to grow.

organic food: food grown on land, free from chemical fertilizers or pesticides.

pesticide: a chemical used to control pests.

pollution: harmful waste substances that affect the air, water or ground.

protein: a chemical made by living organisms which is also used for growth and repair.

renewable: something that can be replaced or regrown, for example trees; or a source of energy that never runs out, such as the sun or wind.

resource: a stock or supply of a material.

sustainable: when something is able to be maintained indefinitely, never running out.

FURTHER INFORMATION

Friends of the Earth UK
26-28 Underwood Street
London, N1 7JQ, UK
Tel: 0171 490 1555

Rare Breed Survival Trust
Royal Agricultural Society
National Agricultural Centre
Stoneleigh, Kenilworth
Warwickshire CV8 2LZ, UK
Tel: 01203 696551

**Soil Association and
British Organic Farmers**
86-88 Colston Street
Bristol, BS1 5BB, UK
Tel: 0117 929 0661

UNICEF – UK
55 Lincoln Inn Fields
London, WC2A 3NB, UK
0171 405 5592

**National Farmers
Association**
GPO Box 1068
Sydney 1041
AUSTRALIA
Tel: 02 9251 1700

**Royal Agricultural
Society of NSW**
Box 4317
GPO Sydney 20001
AUSTRALIA
Tel: 02 9331 9111

UNICEF Australia
9th Floor
55 Clarence Street
Sydney NSW 2000
Tel: 02 9290 2099

INDEX

A

Africa 8, 16, 17, 22, 23
Agenda 21 4, 6, 12, 14, 18,
    20, 26
aid 12, 29
animals 4, 6, 13, 15, 17, 18, 20,
    22, 23, 25
Asia 8
Australasia 6

C

Canada 21
cattle 20, 22, 23
cereals 6, 13, 14, 20, 21
chemicals 6, 7, 8, 9, 12, 14,
    16-17, 27
China 13
climate 4, 15
conservation 11, 25, 26
crops 4, 5, 6, 7, 8, 13, 15, 16,
    17, 18, 19, 22, 24, 25
    cash 29
    failure of 20, 21

D

developed countries 6, 9, 12,
    14, 16, 18, 26, 28
developing countries 8, 9, 12,
    14, 15, 18, 26, 28, 29
diet 4, 15, 17, 20
diseases 7, 16, 21, 23, 25
drought 15, 18, 24

E

Earth Summit 10
environment 5, 6, 7, 8, 9, 11, 12,
    13, 14, 16, 21, 22, 23, 26, 27
Europe 6, 22, 27, 28

F

fair trade 28-29
famine 18, 21
farming methods
    environmentally sensitive
    12, 13, 14

intensive 6, 13
modern 5, 6, 12, 16
traditional 8, 13, 15, 28
fertilizers 7, 14, 16
fish 4, 12, 18, 19
fruit 4, 9, 27
food
    chain 7
    labels 29
    organic 27, 28, 29
    preserving 9
    transportation 9, 12, 27
    variety 12, 20, 21, 24, 25
foreign debt 14, 28, 29

G

genetic engineering 24-25
goats 20, 22
Green Revolution 14, 15, 16

H

harvests 11, 13, 14
Honduras 8

I

India 13, 27
insects 7, 17
Ireland 21
irrigation 18-19

K

Kenya 15, 18, 27

L

land use 5, 6, 21
local food 26, 27, 28, 29

M

machinery 6, 8
maize 8, 15, 24
meat 4, 15, 22, 28
milk 4, 22, 28
minerals 4

N

New Zealand 27
nutrients 7, 16, 18

P

pests 7, 14, 16-17, 24
pollution 7, 14, 18, 27
potatoes 20, 21
protein 4, 19

R

resources
    equal shares of 28
    recycling 16, 18, 29
rice 13
right to food 11, 13
Rwanda 29

S

scientists 7, 12, 15, 24
sheep 20, 22
soil 4, 5, 7, 13, 14, 15, 16
South America 8
Southeast Asia 13

U

UK 17, 21, 27
United Nations 10
United States 6, 21, 27

V

vegetables 4, 8, 9, 27
vitamins 4

W

war 29
waste 12, 15, 18, 26, 27, 29
water 7, 12, 14, 15, 18-19, 26,
    27, 29
wheat 6, 13, 28
wildlife 5, 16

Z

Zaire 15

3 8002 00714 7558